Mummies and Curious Corpses

Natalie Jane Prior wrote *Bog Bodies* because she has always been fascinated by archaeology. Her other interests include gardening, theatre, science fiction, and chocolate. She lives in inner-city Brisbane with her bull terrier, Ragnar.

Natalie has published four other children's books with Allen & Unwin. Her first picture book, *The Paw*, (illustrated by Terry Denton) was shortlisted for the Children's Book Council of Australia Book of the Year Award in 1994.

By the same author:
The Amazing Adventures of Amabel
Amabel Abroad
The Paw
Mysterious Ruins

Bog Bodies

Mummies and Curious Corpses

Natalie Jane Prior

A
LITTLE
ARK
BOOK

ALLEN & UNWIN

First published in 1994

A Little Ark Book
Allen & Unwin Pty Ltd
9 Atchison Street
St Leonards NSW 2065, Australia

National Library of Australia
cataloguing-in-publication entry:

Prior, Natalie Jane, 1963-.
    Bog Bodies mummies and curious corpses

    Bibliography
    Includes index
    ISBN 1 86373 583 6

    1. Bog bodies - Juvenile literature. 2. Mummies - Juvenile literature. 3. Human remains
(Archaeology) - Juvenile literature. I. Title. (Series: True stories (St Leonards, N.S.W.)).

393.3

Designed and typeset by Site Design/Illustration, Melbourne
Set in Century Old Style Regular and Helvetica Condensed
Printed by McPherson's Printing Group, Maryborough, Victoria

10 9 8 7 6 5 4 3

Picture credits:

© Cover image: G. Turner, 1981

Text Illustrations: pages 11, 16 -17, 24, 27, 33, 43, 52, 55, 62, 69, 73, 84 © Nick Abodanza.
All other text illustrations © John Nicholson, except for page 18 (top illustration courtesy of
Austral International) and pages 68 and 70 (*London Illustrated News*)

Austral International: 2/Camera Press/Presna Latina: 8/Sygma: 4/Sygma/Polly Borland: 9
• Coo-ee Historical Picture Library: 5, 6, 7 • Alex Morgan/Museo de las Momias: 3
• South Australian Museum: 16, 17 • Sporting Pix/Popperfoto: 1• Whitehaven Museum,
Cumbria, England/G. Turner, Ravenglass: 10, 11, 12, 13, 14, 15
(numbers refer to the photographs in the colour section)

The publishers would like to thank Harry Fancy AMA of the Whitehaven Museum
(Cumbria, England) and Alex Morgan for their assistance in preparing this book.
Thanks to Catherine O'Rourke for picture research.

Contents

For Kim

Acknowledgements

Many people helped me write this book. I would like to say thank you to my parents, Gordon and Jan Prior for their love and financial support, which enabled the book to be written; Peter Nussey for writing the computer programme that drew the sarcophagus, and putting up with endless months of conversation about preserved people; John Shields, Linda Miller, Maureen Speller and Gill Nussey for generously collecting information; Emma Baker-Spink, for helping design the bog woman's hairstyle; Harry Fancy of the Whitehaven Museum, Cumbria, and John Todd for answering my questions about the St Bees Knight; Kelly Miller from the University of Queensland Central Library Inter-Library Loans Department for her tireless work on my behalf; also the staffs of Logan City Libraries, the Queensland Museum Library, and the State Library of Queensland. Finally, I would like to say thank you to Rosalind Price of Allen & Unwin for asking me to write what has been one of the most fascinating and entertaining projects I have ever undertaken, and to Beth Dolan for seeing it through to fruition.

Introduction

When people and animals die, their bodies immediately begin to decay. Invisible bacteria breed inside and destroy the body's cells. Flies and insects lay eggs which hatch into hungry maggots. The body bursts, the eyes dissolve, and the flesh rots away. Eventually, all that is left is a grinning skeleton.

Sometimes, by accident or because somebody intended it, a dead body does not decay. It can be pickled like olives in vinegar, or frozen like meat in a freezer. Or it can be dried out like a prune or dried apricot. The bacteria which cause decay are killed or discouraged, and the dead body becomes a preserved person.

This book is about dried, pickled and frozen preserved people. Some of them are hundreds, even thousands of years old, yet they appear much as they did when they were alive. By studying them archaeologists, doctors and other experts can learn about the way people lived: the clothes they wore, the food they ate, even the diseases they suffered from. Most importantly, by learning about preserved people and comparing them with modern humans, we can all learn more about ourselves.

1. Bog Bodies

1. Bog Bodies

The people in the peat

For hundreds of years they have been appearing in the marshes of Northern Europe. Their bodies are brown and tanned like leather. Some of them even have fingerprints. Every hair, every toe and fingernail, is perfectly preserved. They are bog bodies—preserved people who died gruesome deaths in the treacherous peat bogs of the north, thousands of years ago.

Bog bodies are some of the most famous preserved people in the world, almost as well known as pop stars and politicians. However, it was not until 1950 that a bog person was examined scientifically by the famous bog body expert, Professor Peter Glob. Professor Glob excavated the Tollund Man from the Danish marsh where he was discovered by peat-cutters and worked with a team of experts to find out as much about him as possible. Professor Glob not only discovered how Tollund Man died and when: he even found out what sort of porridge he had eaten for his last meal!

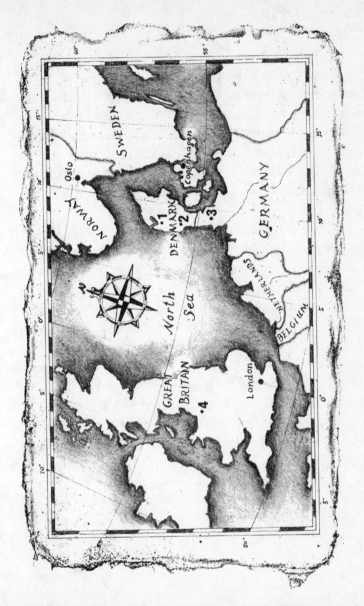

Bog Bodies have been found all over Northern Europe. This map marks sites of some of the famous finds discussed in this book.
1. Grauballe Man. 2. Tollund Man. 3. Windeby Girl. 4. Lindow Man.

Professor Glob also proved that bog bodies owe their remarkable preservation to **peat**. Peat (ancient, decomposed plant matter found in bogs, and burnt as fuel in cold countries) contains a bark extract called **tannin**. When a dead body is placed in a peat bog, the peat cuts off the air supply to the bacteria which would otherwise cause decay. The tannin in the water kills them, and the body is preserved.

Sometimes bog bodies are so miraculously preserved that people refuse to believe they are as old as the experts say. An old lady in Denmark swore that Grauballe Man was her childhood playmate, who had disappeared many years before, even though scientists had dated him to about AD 300. And when a woman's head was found in Lindow Moss, near Manchester in England, in 1983, a local man, Peter Reyn-Bardt, gave himself up to the police. Twenty years ago, he confessed, he had murdered his wife and thrown her body into the Moss. The police arrested him, but the murderer should have held his tongue. Peter Reyn-Bardt was sent to prison—after it was proved that his 'wife' was at least 1700 years old.

The human sacrifice

It had been a bad winter, and people in the village of Windeby, in Iron Age Denmark, had gone hungry. For months Ertha, the goddess of fertility who sent the crops, had ignored their sacrifices and prayers. Now spring was late coming. Everyone knew the goddess was angry, and that only one thing could please her. Ertha was thirsty for the blood of a human sacrifice.

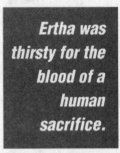

Ertha was thirsty for the blood of a human sacrifice.

The victim was a girl of about thirteen, the daughter of an important villager. She had fair hair which she wore tied back in a red and yellow headband, a delicate face, and small hands and feet. The girl was frightened when they told her what was going to happen, but she knew there was no other choice. If she refused to be the sacrifice, her family and friends would die in the hard times to come.

The girl ate the ritual meal the priests prepared for her, and stood patiently while they shaved her hair. Late at night she was led out to the sacrificial bog. Fires were lit to warm the cold spring night. The last thing the girl saw as the priests bound her eyes was the torchlight flickering on the water of the shallow bog. A moment later they pushed her into the cold water and held her under with tree branches until she drowned.

In 1952 the girl who died on that long-ago night was dug up by peat-cutters in southern Denmark. Her eyes were still bound with her red and yellow headband, and a big stone had been dropped on top of her body to make it sink.

Archaeologists believe the Windeby Girl, like most other bog people, was sacrificed to the goddess in winter or early

spring to make sure crops in the coming year would be fruitful. Because bogs were sacred to the goddess, all sorts of offerings were thrown into them: money and jewellery as well as people. Today, when we throw coins into wishing wells, we are remembering the grisly human sacrifices of the past.

Hair comb found with a Danish bog woman

Because so many bog bodies are well preserved, archaeologists have been able to learn a great deal about the people who were chosen to die. Human sacrifices were usually young, healthy and attractive people. Their hands are smooth and elegant, not rough from hard work, meaning they were people of importance. Iron Age people believed that to offer the goddess a slave or unimportant person would be an insult. To be a human sacrifice was probably a great honour. Some people may even have volunteered. Many bog bodies have calm, peaceful expressions on their faces, and it has been said that Tollund Man looks as if he were asleep!

The human sacrifice's last night on earth began with a ceremonial meal. This was normally some kind of gruel or grain porridge made from whatever plants were available. By examining the contents of a bog body's stomach, botanists can find out exactly how much of each plant was used. In 1954, as part of a television programme, some gruel was made to a recipe based on the contents of the Tollund Man's stomach. It was served to two famous archaeologists, who agreed it tasted disgusting!

After the sacrifice ate his or her meal, a few hours went by. (We know this because the food in bog people's stomachs is usually partly digested.) Then the victim was tied with a rope or leather thong, and his or her clothes were often removed. Except where the victim was drowned, the sacrifice may not have taken place at the actual bog. The ground around bogs is soft and treacherous, so it is likely that the person was killed somewhere safe and dry, and only taken to the bog when already dead.

Woven cap found in a Northern European bog

All of the bog people died violent, even gruesome deaths. Some had their throats cut, or were hanged or strangled with cords. Others were beheaded, stabbed, or drowned. Sometimes more than one method was used. Grauballe Man's skull was smashed in and his throat cut from ear to ear. The most grisly death of all was that of the English bog person, Lindow Man. He was bashed with a club, throttled with a piece of cord *and* had his throat cut!

After the sacrifice, the dead body was thrown into the bog. To stop it floating, it was pinned down with forked sticks or rocks. By morning, apart from some bloodstains and ash marks on the nearby grass, all trace of the sacrifice had disappeared. Life in the village could return to normal—until Ertha once more called out for human blood.

Activity:
The bog woman's hairstyle

Here are instructions for a hairstyle similar to that worn by
Iron Age women at the time of the bog people. It is based on
the hairstyle of a bog body found at Bred Fen in Denmark
in 1942.

This hairstyle will work best on people whose hair is at
least shoulder length. You will need a brush and comb,
bobby pins, four elastic bands, and two lengths of coloured
wool at least twice the length of your hair.

INSTRUCTIONS

1. Part hair down centre.

2. Pull hair upwards into two ponytails, high on the
   sides of the head as shown in the picture. Secure the
   ponytails with two of the elastic bands.

3. Plait each ponytail into a three-strand plait. Secure
   the ends of the plaits with the remaining elastic
   bands.

4. Tuck the end of one of the lengths of wool under the rubber band at the top of one of the plaits. Wind the wool around the elastic band until it is completely covered. Secure the wool by tucking it under the elastic. (You should have a long length of wool dangling beside the plait.)

5. Wind the wool around the plait, all the way down to the second elastic band. Tuck the wool under the elastic and wind it around the band to cover it (see step 4). Secure end of wool by tucking it under the elastic band.

6. Repeat steps 4 and 5 for second plait.

7. Wrap the two plaits around the crown of the head and secure with bobby pins as shown.

The Druid in the Moss

In 1984, while cutting peat at Lindow Moss in Cheshire, England, a workman called Andy Mould saw a strange-looking piece of wood on the conveyor belt. Afraid it might jam the machinery, he picked it up and tossed it to one of his friends.

Lindow Man's head was crushed after centuries under the peat

'Here. Catch!'

The other man turned, but not quite fast enough. The piece of 'wood' hit the ground, showering peat everywhere.

'Quick! Stop the machinery! And call the police!' The second man bent hastily and brushed away the bits of peat. Andy Mould hurried over to see what the matter was. Lying on the ground, mangled, but clearly recognisable, was a human foot.

Murder had been committed—but how long ago? Within hours Rick Turner, the county archaeologist, arrived to take charge of the case. The police were contacted in case the body was that of a recent murder victim, and together the archaeologist and the detectives scoured the bog for clues. Finally Rick Turner spotted a piece of leathery skin poking out of the peat, and the mystery was solved. The body was lying in a layer of peat which was at least 2000 years old.

The body was cut out of the peat and taken to a nearby hospital. Tests were carried out which proved that this was an ancient preserved person, and 'Lindow Man' (or 'Pete Marsh' as he was nicknamed by the newspapers) was handed over to the British Museum for study. The first task here was to free his body from the huge slab of peat which still surrounded it. The museum workers began by X-raying the peat. By using the X-rays as a 'map' they were able to remove the peat without damaging the body. Unfortunately, Lindow Man had been chopped in half at the waist by peat-cutting machinery, and only the top part of his body remained. He had also been badly squashed by the weight of the peat, and his left hand had completely disappeared.

Despite these missing pieces, the 'detectives' at the museum were able to build up a good picture of what Lindow Man had looked like. They discovered he was a young man with brown hair and a beard, and a fit, muscular body. He was probably about 1.68 metres (5 feet 6 inches) tall, although without his legs it is difficult to be sure of his exact height.

Sticks were sometimes used to hold bog people underwater to ensure they drowned

His hands are smooth, and his body unmarked by hard work. Whoever he was, like most bog bodies, Lindow Man was a person of high rank.

The investigators also discovered that Lindow Man died a particularly gruesome death. First, he was hit twice on the back of the head, so hard that the blows fractured his skull. A thong was tied tightly around his neck and was tightened with a stick to strangle him. Finally, his throat was cut. When every last drop of blood had spurted out of him, his naked body was thrown into the bog.

Most experts are sure that Lindow Man was a human sacrifice. They believe that his grisly end had some sort of ritual importance. One 'detective', archaeologist Dr Anne Ross, has pieced the clues together and come up with a possible solution to the mystery.

She thinks Lindow Man was a **Druid**—an ancient Celtic priest-magician—who was sacrificed to the gods after the Celtic queen **Boudicca** was defeated by the Romans in AD 60. The Romans hated the Druids, and tried to stamp them out. Shortly before the defeat of Boudicca, the Druids were completely destroyed by a Roman army on their magical island of Mona off the coast of Wales.

Dr Ross believes Lindow Man made the long journey to Cheshire from Ireland. He arrived in England early in AD 60 and made his way to Lindow Moss, where he was met by a few Druids who had survived the massacre on Mona. Here he was given a special cake made of wheat, rye and barley, burned black to signify he had been picked to die. (The scorched remains of this cake were found in Lindow Man's stomach.) The other Druids sacrificed him, probably at the great Celtic festival of Beltain, and threw his body into Lindow Moss.

Sadly if Dr Ross's theory is true, Lindow Man's sacrifice was in vain. The Romans stayed in Britain for another 400 years. And the Druids' magical power was shattered, never to return.

**Fertility symbol
from the Bronze Age,
found in a bog**

The stuffed philosopher

Medical students dissect human corpses to learn how the body works. Today, it is common for people to will their bodies to science, but this was not always the case. For many years only the bodies of executed criminals could be used for dissection. When there weren't enough dead criminals, the only alternative was to buy a corpse freshly stolen or 'resurrected' from a graveyard by a body snatcher.

One of the first people to will his body to science was the philospher, Jeremy Bentham, who died in 1832. His body was dissected before an audience of his friends. Then, following Bentham's own instructions, the surgeon had it stuffed with straw and mounted in a glass case. Jeremy Bentham now makes his home at University College, London, where he is back on display after a recent visit to the dry-cleaners.

A pickled admiral . . .

After his death at the Battle of Trafalgar, in Spain, Admiral Lord Nelson's body was sent back to England for a hero's funeral. But because Trafalgar was a long way from home, and sailing ships travelled slowly, the admiral's body had to be preserved. Some enterprising sailors remembered that alchohol stops things from rotting, and Lord Nelson duly arrived home—pickled in a barrel of rum. Ever since, sailors have traditionally called a drink of rum 'tapping the admiral'.

A stewed king . . .

When the English King Henry V died in France in 1422, his body was chopped into bits and boiled down in huge vats in the castle kitchens. The bones and flesh were placed in a lead box, seasoned with herbs, and sent back to England to be buried like a human casserole.

A preserved queen . . .

Henry's queen, Katherine de Valois, was left in an open coffin made out of roofing lead for over 200 years. Visitors to Westminster Abbey described her embalmed body as being badly dressed, and having skin like leather.

One visitor was even more disrespectful. After seeing Queen Katherine on his thirty-sixth birthday, the seventeenth-century diarist Samuel Pepys wrote proudly in his diary that he had 'kissed the queen's mouth'!

And an unpreserved one . . .

Decomposing bodies swell up with gas which eventually bursts the skin like a piece of rotten fruit. Queen Elizabeth I was so badly embalmed her body exploded at her funeral and blew up the coffin.

2. The Greenland Mummies

2. The Greenland Mummies

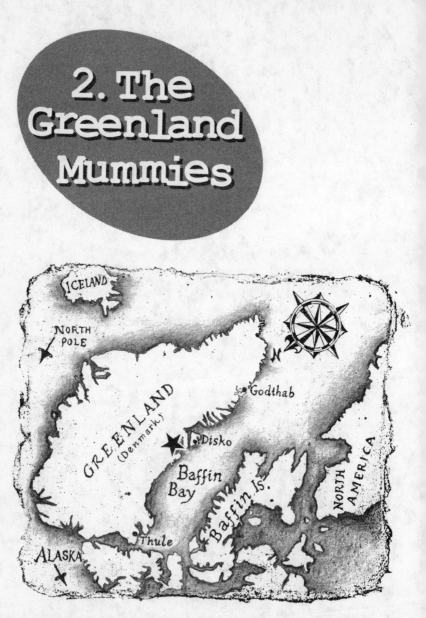

Greenland, showing site ★ where mummies were discovered

The graves of Qilakitsoq

Greenland is one of the world's most northerly countries.
For long months during the winter the sun almost
disappears from its frozen shores. Seals and whales frolic in
its icy waters and fog presses heavily over the deserted
settlement of **Qilakitsoq*** on the western coast. Once, every
winter, Inuit (Eskimos) came here to hunt. Today all that is
left of the settlement are a few ruined houses, and some
lonely graves on the rocky hillside.

In October 1972, two brothers called Hans and Jokum
Grønvold set out on a hunting expedition near the old
Qilakitsoq ruins. While climbing the rugged slopes to the
west of the settlement the brothers spotted two strange, flat
rocks. The rocks did not seem to fit in with their
surroundings. They appeared to have been put there
deliberately. Idly, Hans Grønvold pulled one aside—and
found himself staring at what seemed to be a freshly
dead corpse!

The Grønvolds ran for help, and returned to investigate
with friends. Soon they had uncovered the bodies of a small
boy and three women. The bodies were wrapped in sealskin
and hidden in a stone chamber about a metre deep. Three
more women and some spare clothes were found in a second
grave nearby. The saddest find of all was a small bundle
which looked like a doll. Eyeless, but with a fringe of black
hair still poking out from under a sealskin parka, it was the
shrivelled body of a tiny Inuit baby.

The Grønvold brothers and their friends swore to keep

---

* Pronounced *krilakittork*

their discovery secret. Hans Grønvold took photographs of the find, and hurried to report it to the authorities. But to his disappointment, nobody seemed very interested. The photographs were put away in a file at the Greenland National Museum. Hidden from view, they were forgotten for the next five years.

It seemed as if the mummies would stay in their lonely graves forever. But rescue was on the way. In 1977, a new director was appointed to the museum. Jens Rosing opened the file on the mummies and saw Hans Grønvold's photographs. Here, he realised, was the most important archaeological discovery ever made in Greenland—and his own staff had completely ignored it!

Because of Jens Rosing's lucky discovery, the Greenland mummies were saved for posterity. A team of archaeologists was sent to Qilakitsoq to excavate the graves. Soon the mummies were winging their way to Denmark, a country they never knew existed, for scientific examination and preservation by more than fifty experts.

Activity:
Inuit face painting

One of the most interesting experiments on the Qilakitsoq mummies was carried out by Niels Kromann, a Danish skin specialist. He photographed them with infra-red film, and discovered that all but one of them were tattooed with curving lines on their foreheads, cheeks and chins. Two of the mummies with identical tattoos were probably sisters.

The Inuit had an unusual method of tattooing. They dipped a bone needle with a sinew thread in soot, and literally sewed the tattoo into the face! By pulling the needle under the skin, soot was left to form permanent patterns. A tattoo line measuring five centimetres took about forty tiny stitches to complete and was excruciatingly painful.

Here is a face-painting pattern based on the tattoos of the Greenland mummies. To do the face painting you will need a dark blue or black face-painting stick or blunt eyebrow pencil. **Do not use sharp eyebrow pencils, biros, felt pens or other non-removable inks**. When you have finished, your 'tattoos' can be removed with cold cream, baby oil or make-up remover.

Preserving the Greenland mummies

When the Greenland mummies arrived in Copenhagen in 1979, the Danish researchers were faced with an enormous problem. Naturally, everyone wanted to find out as much information about the mummies as possible. But the Greenland National Museum also wanted them preserved, so they could put them on permanent display. The fragile bodies had to be treated with such care that the researchers could not even remove the mummies' clothes!

Normally, the best way of finding out about a dead person is to cut the body open and do an **autopsy**. In the case of the Greenland mummies, the researchers could not do this because it would have destroyed the bodies and their clothes. So they began by **X-raying** the mummies, and examining their clothed bodies from head to foot. Then they used **carbon dating** to find out exactly how old the mummies were.

Sealskin jacket worn by Qilakitsoq mummy baby

The mummies were probably buried in their rocky graves about AD 1475. Without autopsies, we don't know what most of them died of, but it may have had something to do with the hard lives people in fifteenth-century Greenland led. Qilakitsoq was a winter settlement, used for hunting seals, whales and caribou. The eight women and children in the graves would have died at the bleakest and most difficult time of year. In winter, there was hardly any light, and no fresh plants or vegetables to eat. Old people, children and babies died easily from disease, hunger or cold. The little boy in the first grave may even have been left out deliberately to die. This seems cruel to us, but because he was crippled and would not have lived to adulthood, his parents probably thought it was the kindest thing to do.

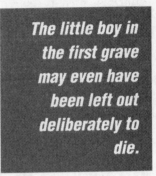

The little boy in the first grave may even have been left out deliberately to die.

Cold winter weather was also responsible for preserving the bodies. Unusual conditions on the hillside where they were buried meant that the mummies were freeze-dried. First, the bodies froze solid like meat in a freezer. Then the winter winds and intense, dry cold sucked the moisture out of them, preserving them so well that two warts were still clearly visible on one mummy's right hand!

The researchers in Copenhagen spent three years discovering all they could about the mummies. Then they turned their attention to the even more important task of preserving them. First, the seventy-eight spare pieces of clothing which were buried with them were soaked in preservative solution, and delicately repaired by experts in ancient clothing. The four best mummies were too big and fragile to be soaked, so it was decided to treat them with gamma radiation. The mummies were wrapped in cheesecloth and plastic, carefully placed in cardboard boxes, and delivered to a radiation plant. Here, in a special irradiation room, they were given a strong dose of radiation. This killed all the bacteria and fungus which might otherwise have caused them to decay.

The preserved mummies were sent back to Greenland in sealed boxes, where they were unpacked in a germ-free environment and put into glass cases. They can now be seen on display in their rightful home: the Greenland National Museum.

D-I-Y mummies

In the eleventh and twelfth centuries, Japanese priests practised a bizarre form of do-it-yourself mummification—while still alive!

The priest gradually ate less and less over a period of years. Then he stopped eating altogether and waited for death, surrounded by large candles intended to draw moisture from his body. Following his death from starvation, his corpse was walled up in an underground room for three years. Then he was brought out and subjected to further candle-drying to finish off the mummification.

3. Ancient Egyptian Mummies

3. Ancient Egyptian Mummies

The Egyptian way of death

No preserved people are more famous than Egyptian mummies. For thousands of years the world has marvelled at these mysterious time travellers, asleep in granite coffins in their tombs and pyramids. But why did the ancient Egyptians go to so much trouble to preserve their dead? And why did they spend their whole lives planning for the moment when they too, would be turned into a mummy?

The ancient Egyptians believed that when a person died, their **ka**, or soul, lived on. But the ka needed a body in which to live. In Egypt's hot climate dead bodies quickly rotted away. Only one type of body did not decay. When a body was buried in the hot desert west of the Nile, the heat in the sand sucked all the moisture out of it. Its flesh and skin shrivelled up and its face sank in over its skull, but it still looked— barely—like a person.

Ancient Egyptians realised that here was a way to preserve their dead for eternity. For centuries they tried to

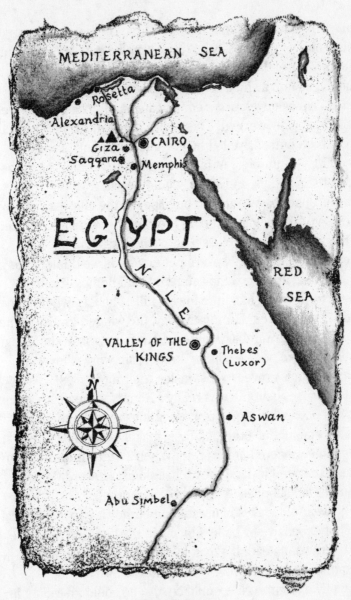

Ancient Egypt

copy the sand-dried mummies. At first, their experiments were not very successful. Without the hot sand to draw out the moisture, the mummies rotted away beneath the bandages into a smelly sludge. But eventually Egyptian **embalmers** developed a complicated and gruesome process which actually worked. The bodies of the dead were turned into dried out, shrivelled husks, filled with bones and stuffing—mummies. At last the ancient Egyptians could be sure their bodies, and souls, would be safe.

Because they wanted to be happy in the afterlife, well-to-do Egyptians began planning their tombs years in advance. They knew that as well as a body, their ka would need a home. Egyptian tombs were not graves as we think of them, but special underground rooms or mini-homes. Their cemeteries were like little towns, full of houses where only dead people lived. During the day, the winged ghosts of the dead left their tombs to flutter about the world of the living. At night, like people coming home from work, they went back to their graves to rest inside their mummies.

Because the tomb was really a home for the dead person, it was filled with everyday possessions to make their afterlife comfortable. Furniture, clothes, make-up, jewellery, toys and even meals were left for them. When **Tutankhamun's** tomb was excavated in 1922 the archaeologist Howard Carter found food supplies of dried beef, mummified ducks, and 3000-year-old loaves of bread! Sometimes it was impractical to put expensive or bulky objects in the tomb, so a picture was drawn instead. If a man had enjoyed boating, for example, a wall-painting which showed him sailing happily along the Nile would ensure he could go sailing in the afterlife.

The Egyptians also filled their tombs with little models of people, which would magically come to life and work as servants. (This was kinder, and more practical than burying real servants alive.) And in case the dead person should be lonely, a favourite pet was sometimes killed and mummified to keep its owner company. The priestess Maat-ka-re was buried with a tiny mummy which many people believed was her baby—until X-rays finally proved it was her pet baboon.

Model servants were placed in Egyptian tombs to serve the dead

Recipe:
Egyptian funerary bread

The ancient Egyptians believed that dead people, like living ones, needed to be fed. After a person died, the family visited the tomb every day with food for his or her soul. Here is a recipe for some date bread similar to that found by archaeologists in ancient Egyptian tombs.

INGREDIENTS
2 cups self-raising flour
$1/2$ cup milk
$1/4$ cup water
$1/2$ cup chopped dates
pinch salt

1. Preheat the oven to 200°C (400°F).
2. Sift the flour with the pinch of salt.
3. Put the flour into a mixing bowl, and make a little well in the middle with your fingers.
4. Mix in the milk and water with a knife. (The mixture should have a slightly crumbly texture. If it is sloppy you will need to add more flour.)
5. Add chopped dates and mix thoroughly.
6. Grease a baking tray with butter or margarine, and shake flour over it evenly. Shape your funerary bread into a round loaf and cut two slits on the top.

7. Bake the bread in the oven for ten to fifteen minutes. Turn the oven down to 180°C (350°F) and bake for another ten minutes. Tap the bread carefully: when it sounds hollow it is cooked.

Food for mummies can be rather dry for living humans. Your Egyptian funerary bread will taste best if eaten with butter and honey (an Egyptian favourite) while still warm.

How a mummy was prepared

Most people, when they think of a mummy, imagine a faceless figure shrouded in bandages, lying in a sarcophagus with its hands folded across its chest. Sometimes, in books or movies, the mummy comes to life in its coffin and grabs the throat of an explorer who has penetrated its tomb, or runs down corridors after beautiful young women. Few people realise that the real mummy—the dried up corpse of a long-dead Egyptian—is *underneath* the bandages. What is most remarkable about it is not any supernatural power, but the amazing process which keeps the body preserved for thousands of years.

When an important ancient Egyptian died his or her body was quickly delivered to the embalmers, who began a lengthy and gruesome ritual aimed at preserving it for eternity. First, they ceremonially washed and cleansed the body in a section of the embalmers' workshop called the **ibu** ('tent of purification'). Then they took it to the **wabet** ('place of embalming'), where they removed the brain. The embalmers did this by sticking a metal probe (like a crochet hook) up the nose and wriggling it around until the brain was stirred into a semi-liquid mush.

Hooks used to pull brains out

Then they tipped the body up, and dribbled the brain porridge out through the nostrils. To complete this stage of the mummification process, the face of the dead person was usually painted with a coating of hot **resin**. This helped preserve the features, and was the first of many coats painted on before embalming was complete.

Next, the embalmers turned their attention to the inside of the body. A special embalmer called the 'slicer' or 'ripper-up' made a slit in the dead person's side or groin with a flint knife. He then inserted his hand and arm to the elbow, and slowly pulled out the stomach, intestines and other organs. The heart, as the most important organ, was left in place, or put back later in the mummification process. When all the organs were removed, the body cavity was washed out and packed with stuffing. It was now ready for the most important step of all: the drying out.

Stone knife

The key ingredient in mummification was a salt called **natron**, which consists largely of sodium bicarbonate (used now in baking powder, to make cakes rise). For many years, Egyptologists argued whether natron was used wet or dry. Some believed bodies were left to soak in huge baths full of natron solution, while others thought they were covered or packed with natron salt and left on racks to dry. By a process of trial and error, using dead animals and amputated human limbs, scientists proved that dead rats soaked in a natron solution actually decayed faster than normal, leaving a stinking soup. But rats buried in dry natron emerged almost perfectly preserved, because the moisture in their bodies was absorbed by the salt.

It took forty days in dry natron for the body to be preserved as a mummy. (Less than this, and the mummy tended to decay. Longer, and it began to fall apart.) At the end of this time, the desiccated corpse was transferred from the wabet to the **per nefer**, or 'house of beauty'. Here it was massaged with sweet-smelling oils and restuffed with linen,

straw, sawdust or even mud. The slit
in the side was sealed with a metal
plate marked with the **udjat-eye**, a
powerful **amulet**. The real eyes
were pushed back into the head and
the sockets filled with bits of linen,
false eyes, or even small onions.

Finally, the body was painted from head to foot
with hot resin, and coated with **ochre**, red for men, yellow
for women.

The last stage of the embalmer's work, and one of the
most complicated, was the wrapping. This took at least two
weeks, and was accompanied by complicated prayers and
rituals. The embalmers began by wrapping each finger and
toe, then the arms and legs, and finally the torso. Each layer
of wrappings contained
protective amulets and
jewellery, and was covered
with hot resin. To save
money, mummy bandages
were often cut up from old

household linen given by the dead person's
family. Very wealthy families, however, could
afford bandages which were specially woven.
One mummy examined in the United States
had 845 square metres of wrappings — that's
the equivalent of 250 ordinary tablecloths!

By the time the **funerary mask** was placed
over the head, and the whole corpse wrapped in
a shroud, the finished mummy looked much like
the bandaged monsters you see in horror films.

But what did it look like underneath its wrappings? The answer is, quite horrific. Because all the moisture in the body had gone, the dead person was often reduced in weight by as much as 75 per cent. Their arms and legs were little more than bony sticks, their flesh sunken in over their skeleton. (The internal organs were preserved separately in a set of four **canopic jars**, like thermos flasks with lids in the shape of animal or human heads.) Their skin was hard, brittle and discoloured, and if the embalming was not properly carried out, the whole mummy crumbled or disintegrated. But in the best, most successful cases it is still possible to look on a mummy and recognise the faces of people dead for thousands of years—just as the ancient Egyptians intended.

Canopic jars

The fishy pharaohs

When the mummies of forty ancient Egyptian pharaohs were discovered at Deir el Bahri in 1881 and shipped to Cairo for study, customs officials demanded the archaeologists pay customs duty on them. Because there was no rate listed for mummies, the pharaohs were charged at the rate for dried fish!

Tomb robbers

Soon after the discovery of Tutankhamun's tomb in 1922, Lord Carnarvon, the man who paid for its excavation, died of pneumonia in Cairo. At the exact moment of his death, all the electric lights in Cairo mysteriously went out. Immediately it was rumoured that Lord Carnarvon had been punished for disturbing the pharaoh's rest. When other people who had worked on the excavation also died, stories began circulating that they, like Lord Carnarvon, were the victims of Tutankhamun's Curse.

Today, hardly anybody believes in the Curse of Tutankhamun. We know that Lord Carnarvon had been in poor health for some time before his death, and that the 'curse' was invented by journalists looking for an exciting story. But magical curses *were* used by wealthy ancient Egyptians as a weapon against tomb robbers, just as tomb builders tried everything they could think of to keep robbers away from defenceless mummies. Because masses of gold and silver treasure was buried with wealthy Egyptians, their tombs were in constant danger of being broken into. No matter how hard tomb builders tried to make the tombs secure, the robbers were always one step ahead of them.

Ancient Egyptian tomb robbers were cunning, brave and resourceful. They tunnelled through solid rock, cut new entry passages from neighbouring tombs, and found their way through complicated mazes of false passages and empty rooms. They avoided booby traps, including deep pits, and sand falls designed to bury them alive. Their work was hard and dangerous. Sometimes tomb roofs collapsed on them: one robber at Riqqa was crushed flat by several tonnes of rock in the very act of stealing a mummy from its coffin. Often a robber would spend long hours secretly digging through rock, only to find that somebody else had robbed the tomb before him. If he was caught, he faced hideous tortures and death by being impaled on a sharp stake. But the treasure he found when he was successful made all the danger and hard work worthwhile.

Although almost all Egyptian tombs were robbed, the most daring robberies took place in the tombs of the pharaohs. (The fabulous treasure found in the tomb of an unimportant pharaoh like Tutankhamun helps us understand just how much royal tomb robbers stood to gain.) By the

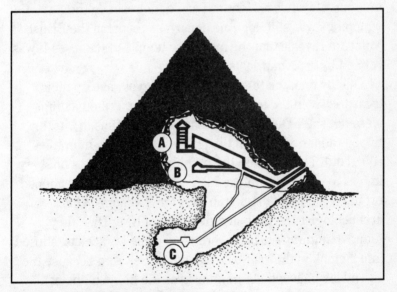

Section of the Great Pyramid at Giza
A   King's Chamber
B   Queen's Chamber
C   Unfinished chamber

time of the New Kingdom (around 1550 BC), the pharaohs realised that the grand pyramid tombs of the past were easy targets. Not one pyramid survived without being robbed. Today, visitors to the **Great Pyramid of Cheops** actually enter through a passage hacked out by robbers.

To trick the robbers, the pharaohs started building secret tombs in the cliffs of the **Valley of the Kings**. But it was impossible to keep the tombs completely hidden, and it was not long before the robbers were back at work. Today, Egyptologists believe many robberies were carried out by cemetery guards, grave-diggers or members of the burial parties. Embalmers stole magic jewelled amulets from the mummy of Princess Henttawi while the resin on the wrappings was still hot. And a papyrus report in the British Museum reveals that the mortuary temple of Rameses II was robbed by its own priests!

One by one, the tombs of ancient Egypt gave up their treasure. Even the mummies in their huge granite coffins were not safe. The robbers smashed the coffins to bits, or tipped them over so that the lids fell off and the mummies rolled out. They hacked the mummies up with axes or sharp knives to get at valuable amulets, and carried away chopped off hands and feet to unwrap later for jewellery. When archaeologists investigated the tomb of King Djer, they found a mummy's arm, covered in jewelled bracelets, stuffed into a crack in the wall by a fleeing robber. And because the Egyptians believed the mummy was the home of the soul, tomb robbers often burned mummies to stop the dead person from haunting them. In one robbery at Thebes, robbers set fire to children's mummies and used them as grisly torches to light their work.

Other mummies met an even more undignified fate. In the sixteenth and seventeenth centuries, thousands of stolen mummies were ground into powder and shipped to Europe—as medicine! At this time, it was quite normal to go to a chemist and ask for extract of mummy to heal cuts and bruises and mend broken bones. Enterprising Egyptians set up special 'mummy factories' to mummify the bodies of executed criminals or beggars, who had often died of horrible diseases such as smallpox. Later, when doctors realised that mummy medicine often caused their patients more harm than good, these fake mummies were sold to wealthy and eccentric Europeans, who collected them as unusual ornaments for their houses.

'Extract of mummy' was crushed to make medicine

Even in modern times Egyptian tombs have not been safe from robbers. In fact it was a modern tomb robber, Mohammed Abd el Rassul, who made one of the most important archaeological discoveries of all time. In 1881, while searching for treasure, he discovered the mummies of forty Egyptian kings and queens which had been hidden from ancient tomb robbers 3000 years before. And in 1969, archaeologists investigating a tomb at Giza found the dead body of a robber, his hand still reaching into an open sarcophagus. He might have been lying there for thousands of years—except that his coat pocket contained a newspaper dated 1944!

Activity:

Cut-out sarcophagus

Wealthy ancient Egyptians were buried in not one, but several coffins. The innermost coffin or mummy case was roughly the shape of the body. It was made of wood, or even a special cardboard called **cartonnage**, and painted with a picture of the dead person. Sometimes a dead person had more than one mummy case, but the outermost coffin was always a heavy **sarcophagus** made out of stone, often granite.

'Nest' of mummy cases for a wealthy Egyptian

A sarcophagus was usually rectangular, though sometimes it was human shaped. It could be very beautiful, and was often carved with hieroglyph spells or passages from the Egyptian **Book of the Dead**. The most important thing was that it should be strong. A solid sarcophagus could mean the difference between tomb robbers destroying the mummy, or not.

This cut-out sarcophagus can be used to store sweets, jewellery, secret messages or any other small item. If you have access to a photocopier which makes enlargement copies you can blow the pattern up and make big ones to hold pens and pencils, or even a doll. However, if you want to use it to hold heavy objects, you may need to paste your photocopy onto a piece of card to give it extra strength.

INSTRUCTIONS

1. Enlarge the pattern on a photocopier below and stick it onto cardboard if desired.
2. Colour or decorate the sarcophagus with felt pens, crayons, glitter or whatever else you like. (Gold and silver metallic pens look fantastic, but be careful the ink doesn't go through the paper.)
3. Cut the sarcophagus out, being careful to cut the angles and corners exactly as they are drawn. (If you don't, your sarcophagus won't fit together properly.) Cut the small slit on the side with a hobby knife.
4. Fold carefully along the lines, making sharp creases. Stick the tabs to the opposite corners as indicated by the arrows. Close the lid by pushing the side tab into the slit.

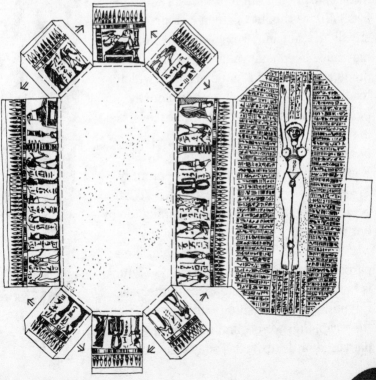

A girl called 1770

One day in ancient Egypt, about 1000 BC, a young girl met with an accident. We don't know exactly what happened to her. Perhaps she was run over by a chariot, or trapped in a building which collapsed. At any rate her injuries were serious, and within a short space of time she died.

Today this ancient Egyptian girl is known by her museum catalogue number—Mummy 1770. Although we are not sure of her real name, or even exactly where she lived, we do have a surprising number of facts about her life. 1770 was about thirteen or fourteen when she died, and came from a wealthy family. She may have been an invalid, living on a diet of fluids, and she had a sinus problem which made breathing difficult for her. Shortly before her death, she lost both her lower legs in some sort of accident. We know this because of the exciting work done by Dr Rosalie David of the Manchester Mummy Project. Every fact we have about 1770 has been learned from a detailed examination of her mummy.

A bandaged mummy looks rather like a parcel waiting to be opened. What, or who, is hidden under the bandages? In the past, Egyptologists found it difficult to resist untying the wrappings to see, and many mummies were damaged or destroyed. Today, because

Mummy 1770

1 The body of Tollund Man was found in Denmark in the 1950s, 2000 years after he was thrown into a peat bog. The noose used to strangle him was still around his neck, and his leather cap was still on his head

2 The 2300-year-old body of Lindow Man awaits autopsy by experts in a London laboratory

3 An eerie mummified body from Mexico

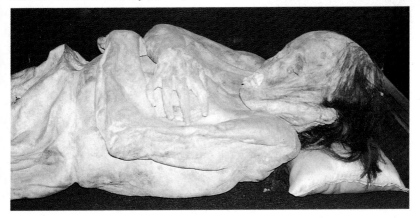

4 The Iceman soon after his discovery in September 1991

5 The mummy case of a priestess of Amon-ra from about 1600 BC

6 The mummified head of Rameses II ('the Great'; ruler from 1279 - 1212 BC), thought to [be] the Pharaoh of the Exodus. During the mummification process, his prominent nose w[as] filled with peppercorns to ensure he kept his noble profile after death

THE PROFILE OF RAMESES II.
(*From a photograph taken at Bûlâk.*)

7 'Examining a mummy': archaeologists at work in the 1860s

8 A *tsantsa* (shrunken head) of the Jivaro tribe from Ecuador. These gruesome artefacts are worn around the necks of warriors on special occasions

9 'Frozen for the future': Thomas Donaldson of Alcor Life Extension with a refrigeration box

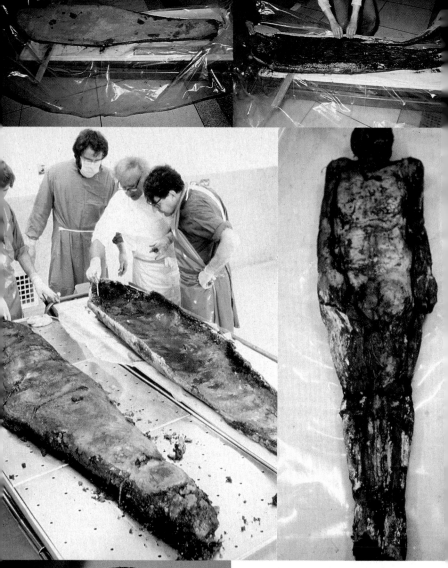

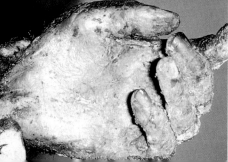

10. – 15. Immediately after his discovery, the St Bees knight was rushed to the morgue of the nearby West Cumberland Hospital. Eddie Tapp, an expert in preserved people, performed an autopsy on the knight—almost 800 years after his death!

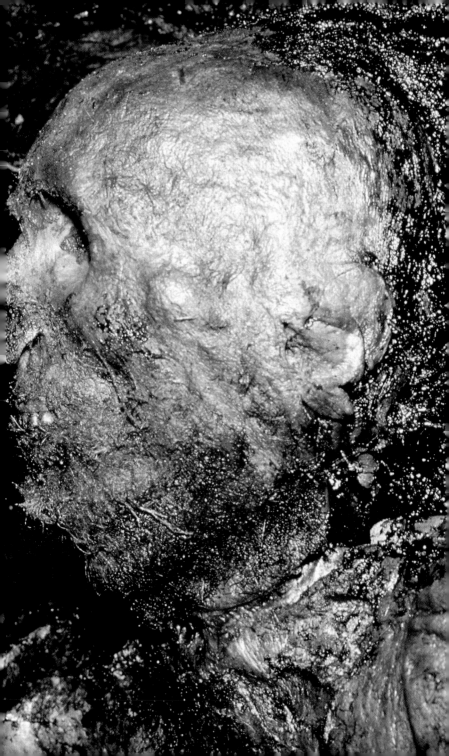

16. 17. George French Angas was an anthropologist and explorer of the 1840s who wrote about the Aboriginals of the Murray mouth in South Australia. This sketch shows mummification of warriors killed in battle as practised by the people of that region:

'The corpses of the young men who have been killed are set up cross-legged on a platform...the arms are extended by means of sticks, the head is fastened back, and all apertures of the body are sewn up; the hair is plucked off, and the fat of the body, which has previously been taken out, is now mixed with red ochre, and rubbed all over the corpse. Fires are then kindled under the platform...

After the body has remained several weeks upon the platform, it is taken down and buried; the skull becoming the drinking cup of the nearest relation. Bodies thus preserved have the appearance of mummies; there is no sign of decay...'

X-rays and other modern medical techniques have made it possible to learn about mummies without taking off the bandages, mummies are rarely unwrapped. When Dr David unwrapped 1770 in 1975, the event was followed by people all over the world.

Dr David and her team of experts planned the unwrapping carefully. First 1770's mummy was X-rayed from head to foot, to give them some idea of what was inside. Then, bit by bit, the bandages were removed. A photographer took pictures of each layer of wrappings—which turned out to be full of 2000-year-old dead beetles! Each insect, and every piece of bandage was carefully put into a plastic bag for further study. At last Dr David removed the gold-painted face mask to reveal 1770 herself, lying with her arms crossed over her chest.

As the researchers had expected from the X-rays, 1770's mummy was in very poor condition. Her flesh was dry and crumbly, and her head was badly damaged. Because her own legs had been lost in the accident, the embalmers had made false ones, and strapped them to the exposed bones. (They did this so her body would be complete in the afterlife, and also to make the mummy look better.) They had even made false feet out of mud

> **Because her own legs had been lost in the accident, the embalmers had made false ones, and strapped them to the exposed bones.**

and reeds, and covered them in pretty decorated slippers, similar to the ones 1770 would have worn when she was alive.

Many of 1770's bones were broken, but researchers were unable to tell whether they had been broken before her death, or later, when her mummy was attacked by tomb robbers and rewrapped. However, because of the poor condition of the mummy, they felt sure that 1770's body had already started to decompose when it was delivered to the embalmers. This would make sense if 1770 had died in an accident. If she had been killed when a building collapsed, for example, it might have taken some time to dig her body out of the rubble.

The unwrapping and autopsy took three people thirty hours to complete. When it was finished, pieces of 1770's bones were given to scientists for carbon dating tests. These revealed that she lived about 3000 years ago, when Egypt was ruled by the Pharaohs of the Twenty-First Dynasty. Some experts have even suggested she might have been a member of the royal family. We certainly know from her beautiful face mask and gold fingernail covers that she came from a wealthy family who loved her and wanted the best for her. Whoever she was, and wherever she was buried, 1770 would have had a grand tomb, containing everything to make her happy in the afterlife.

However, at some time in the past robbers broke into 1770's tomb. They stole her grave treasure, and damaged her mummy so badly that around AD 300 it had to be rewrapped. The people who did the rewrapping did not know who 1770 was. But they knew she must have come from an important family, so they took great care over their work. They replaced the gold fingernail covers stolen by the robbers and used good quality material for the bandages. The mummy was in such bad condition that they were not sure whether it was a girl or boy. So as well as gold nipple covers for a girl, they provided it with an artificial penis made out of rolled up bandages.

The most exciting part of the investigation was still to come. When Dr David finished unwrapping 1770, she called in Richard Neave, an artist who specialised in making models of people's faces from their skulls. Piece by piece, he put 1770's broken skull together like a jigsaw. A cast was made, and a face was modelled over it in clay. A final, wax version was made and dressed in a wig and make-up similar to those a 13-year-old Egyptian girl would have worn. For the first time in nearly 3000 years, the researchers saw what 1770 really looked like—a pretty girl with a round face and almond shaped eyes.

The lost people of Pompeii

Some of the strangest preserved people are not really preserved at all. The citizens of Pompeii, an ancient Roman town, disappeared when their city was buried by a volcano in AD 79.

Years later, archaeologists excavating the site found it riddled with strange hollows. The archaeologists filled the hollows with plaster, then chipped away the rock to reveal the contorted shapes of Pompeii's lost inhabitants. Buried by slowly hardening ash, their bodies had rotted away, leaving only a mould in the rock.

Dozens of men, women and children were found, preserved at the very moment of their deaths. Saddest of all was a dog, still chained to a wall in one of the villas. Its owners had forgotten it in their haste to escape, and it had died alone, choked by the deadly rain of ash.

Sunday afternoon mummies

In the nineteenth century, unwrapping mummies was a favourite Sunday afternoon entertainment. Members of the public could buy tickets to special 'unrollings'—and even take away pieces of the mummy's bandages as souvenirs!

LORD LONDESBOROUGH
AT HOME,
MONDAY 10th JUNE, 1850
144 PICCADILLY.

A Mummy from Thebes to be unrolled at half-past Two

To .... No ....

4. The Iceman

4. The Iceman

The fabulous frozen man

On 19 September 1991, some German climbers on holiday in the Alps made an extraordinary discovery. While walking along the Similaun Glacier, Erika Simon and her husband Helmut caught sight of something sticking out of the ice. Helmut Simon thought it looked like a doll's head. The Simons went over to inspect it, and realised they had found the head and shoulders of a human body!

The Simons reported their find to the police, who promised to investigate. Nobody realised yet just how important the body on the glacier was. A few curious people went to look at it, and later a policeman arrived in a helicopter. He tried to free the body from the ice with a jackhammer, and damaged it badly in the process.

The body lay on the glacier for five days. Finally a forensic expert, Dr Rainer Henn, arrived from Innsbruck University. By this time people exploring the site had discovered an ancient axe and a stone knife. Dr Henn took one look and

Ötzi was found 93 metres inside the Italian border. Austria and Italy both claim the right to his body.

realised the body was not a modern person who had lost his way and become frozen in the ice, but an ancient preserved person. This was not a job for the detectives, but for the archaeologists.

Dr Henn called in his colleague, Professor Konrad Spindler, an expert in prehistory. Professor Spindler examined the axe and the body, and confirmed that the 'Iceman' was at least 4000 years old. (Later, scientists at Oxford University proved that he was actually 5300 years old.) The professor took the Iceman's body with him to Innsbruck University. Here it was treated for growths of fungus and stored in a special cold room at minus six degrees Celsius. While the Austrian researchers found a pet name for him, 'Ötzi' (after the Ötzaler Alps where he was found), archaeologists on the glacier excavated arrows, a cape and other artefacts belonging to the Iceman's climbing kit.

Flint knife found near the Iceman's body

As soon as news of the discovery became widely known, people all over the world went Ötzi crazy. Ötzi's face appeared on television, and on the covers of newspapers and magazines. Ötzi-shaped sweets started appearing in shops near the place where he was found, and someone wrote a song about him. One woman even offered to have Ötzi's baby! Meanwhile, an argument developed between the Italian and Austrian authorities as to who 'owned' Ötzi's body. A survey revealed he had died 92.6 metres on the Italian side of the border. Italian researchers accused the Austrians of 'kidnapping' Ötzi, and demanded they give his body back.

However, work on Ötzi had already become an international affair. Specialists in botany, glaciology, prehistory, and anatomy arrived in Austria to examine him. By studying a prehistoric person and his possessions, they hoped to learn what early European people were like. Ötzi is important because he died accidentally while going about his normal business. For the first time, archaeologists and prehistorians have been able to see artefacts such as copper axes as they were used in everyday life.

While nobody knows exactly how Ötzi came to be buried under the glacier, experts now believe that freak weather conditions, and pure good luck, preserved him for so long before revealing him again. Following his death in the rocky crevice, his body was completely dried out by cold, sun and a hot dry wind known as the Föhn. It was then covered by snow, which froze what was left of it under the moving glacier. Protected by the rocks, Ötzi lay there for over 5000 years until the glacier began to shrink.

Shortly before the discovery in 1991, an unusual amount of dust blew across from the Sahara, and settled on the ice. This made the ice melt more quickly, at centimetres a day. Eventually, the ice surrounding Ötzi melted away, and Europe's visitor from the past was uncovered for the first time in 5000 years.

Freeze-drying experiment

The Iceman was preserved by a combination of freezing and drying out. To see how the **freeze-drying** process works, take a small sliver of raw meat and put it in the freezer without any covering. After a few days the frozen meat will become whitish in colour. The dry cold in the freezer has frozen the meat, and sucked all the moisture out of it.

Frozen mammoths

In Siberia, in north-eastern Russia, snap-frozen woolly mammoths have been found in icy crevasses, where they have lain hidden for 30 000 years. In one case, the mammoth was so fresh that its flesh was carved into steaks and used to feed sled dogs!

Who was the Iceman?

As soon as the Iceman was discovered, people all over the world began wondering who he was. Was he a hunter or shepherd, caught out in a snow storm, or a trader who had lost his way while crossing the Alps? Where had he come from, and where was he going? How had he died, and when? A careful study of Ötzi and his possessions is already beginning to give us the answers.

Some questions can be answered easily. Ötzi was in his late twenties, with swarthy skin, a beard, and dark hair neatly trimmed into the world's oldest haircut. He was quite short—about 1.6 metres—and was tattooed on his back, knee and ankle with lines and crosses. He was well dressed for the cold in a grass cape, leather jacket and trousers, a fur hat and boots stuffed with hay. Ötzi was extremely well equipped for his day. His climbing kit included a copper axe, rope, a leather pouch with a scraper in it, an unstrung bow, and a fur quiver full of unfinished arrows. His backpack contained food supplies including a ripe sloe or plum. This suggests that he probably died in autumn. Whatever he was doing in the Alps, it is clear Ötzi's trip was carefully planned.

Historians believe that Ötzi may have come from one of two different areas of settlement, one in northern Italy between Milan and Venice, the other in southern Switzerland and Austria. Prehistoric villages there were usually built on the edges of lakes. People lived by hunting and simple farming. (Ötzi's worn

Otzi's axe

teeth show he ate a lot of coarse grain.) Perhaps the Iceman was travelling from one area to the other. At any rate, some time in a long-forgotten prehistoric autumn, he took shelter among the rocks of the Similaun Glacier. Here, overcome by cold, a snow storm or perhaps even ill health, he died.

Although we will probably never know exactly who Ötzi

> **Although we will probably never know exactly who Ötzi was, the most romantic theory is that he was a shaman or witchdoctor.**

was, the most romantic theory is that he was a **shaman** or witchdoctor. A number of curious details support this idea. First, the fact that he was carrying a copper axe at a time when most people had only stone means that Ötzi was a person of great importance. Only a chieftain, or a respected priest-magician could be expected to have what was, in 3300 BC, such new technology. Second, mountains are traditionally sacred. The Iceman's body was found quite close to a place still regarded in local folklore as a holy site. The fact that Ötzi's weapons were virtually useless (the arrows, for example, had no tips) suggests that they were for rituals, rather than hunting or fighting. And finally, the mushrooms in his pouch—which experts initially thought were tinder for lighting fires—were powerful **hallucinogens**, eaten to induce visions of gods, spirits, or perhaps even the future.

5. The Mysterious Medieval Knight

5. The Mysterious Medieval Knight

United Kingdom, showing site ★ where the St Bees knight was discovered

The St Bees man

One of the loneliest and most beautiful places in north-west England is St Bees Head, on the coast of Cumbria. Seabirds whirl above its red sandstone cliffs and the village of St Bees, where an old priory was once dedicated to an ancient Irish princess. The monks who lived here are long gone, but for six hundred years, a most unusual preserved person lay hidden in a secret **vault** under their church.

In 1981 an archaeologist called Deirdre O'Sullivan was digging in a demolished section of the old St Bees church. Her excavations had already uncovered the skeletons of many medieval monks when she noticed a strange slope in the ground where she was working. The slope led her to a sandstone **crypt** or vault set into the ground near what was once the altar of the church.

Deirdre O'Sullivan climbed down into the crypt to investigate. Lying on its dusty floor was a skeleton, and the rotted remains of an ancient wooden coffin. She grew very excited. Although only a few rusted fastenings were left of the wooden coffin, beneath the clay packing which had filled it she could see a second, lead coffin in the shape of a human body. Lead coffins of this type had not been used since early

Two shrouds were removed—to reveal the open mouth and staring eyes of a medieval knight!

medieval times, around AD 1300. Whose body could the coffin contain? The coffin was taken to the surface, where it was cut open. Two shrouds were removed—to reveal the open mouth and staring eyes of a medieval knight!

The knight was dated to the fourteenth century. Still in his lead coffin, he was rushed to the morgue of the nearby West Cumberland Hospital. Dr Eddie Tapp, a specialist in preserved people who also worked on Mummy 1770 was brought in to do an autopsy. As soon as his scalpel sliced through the knight's skin what seemed to be fresh red blood flowed from the wound!

> **As soon as his scalpel sliced through the knight's skin what seemed to be fresh red blood flowed from the wound!**

Not only his eyes, but his hair, fingernails, and internal organs were all completely intact. Strangest of all, around his neck was a long piece of woman's hair, obviously given to him as a keepsake by someone he loved.

Dr Tapp's autopsy showed the St Bees knight was about forty years old when he died. He had been killed in some sort of fight. His jaw was fractured in two places and one of his ribs was broken, as if somebody had knocked him off his warhorse. The sharp end of the broken rib had pushed into his right lung. Blood from this wound filled the lung cavity. Eventually the knight's right lung collapsed, and unable to breathe, he died.

Because the St Bees knight had no tombstone no one is really sure who he was. However, experts who have studied him have made some suggestions. They think he probably died in the Middle East because pollen from that region was found on his shroud. Medieval people who had done something wrong often went to the Holy Land on dangerous and difficult journeys called **pilgrimages**. The St Bees knight may have been a pilgrim as he was wearing a special rope called a **penitent's noose** around his neck to show he was sorry for what he had done.

The St Bees knight may also have been a crusader, who travelled to the Holy Land to drive the Muslims out of Jerusalem. If this is the case, he could have died there in battle and been sent home for burial. Dr John Todd, an historian who helped Deirdre O'Sullivan in her investigations, thinks the knight may have been a Cumbrian nobleman called Anthony de Lucy. Anthony de Lucy was about the same age as the knight when he died. He had a wife, and a sister called Maud, either of whom could have given him the lock of hair. And finally, he is known to have travelled to Eastern Europe as a crusader, and may easily have gone to the Holy Land as well.

How had the St Bees knight been so miraculously preserved? The answer is simple, and can be found in almost any modern cookbook. Today, when people make jam they often pour a layer of hot wax over the top of it to seal it against the air. The people who prepared the St Bees man for burial did something very similar. They wrapped his body in a special shroud called a **cerecloth**, and coated it in a sticky beeswax mixture. The wax, the shroud, and the lead coffin shut out all the air—and with it, the bacteria which cause decay.

Mushroom ketchup

Before archaeologists existed, much of their work was done by people called **antiquaries**. Antiquaries were often rather eccentric people who liked to surround themselves with mouldy books and manuscripts, and spend their holidays digging up ancient ruins.

One antiquary by the name of White had the good fortune to dig up a preserved person. In 1779, at Danbury in Essex, he discovered the body of a medieval knight, buried in a thick lead coffin. The knight was lying in a pool of liquid which the antiquary tasted. He reported it was a 'pickle somewhat resembling mushroom ketchup'.

Boiled villians

In England in the sixteenth and seventeenth centuries, the executioner often doubled as a cook! After each execution, he took the severed heads away to a special kitchen and boiled them in a big kettle with salt (to preserve them) and cumin (a herb which made them taste bad to birds). The boiled heads were spiked on long poles and displayed on London Bridge as a warning to other wrongdoers.

6. The Franklin Expedition

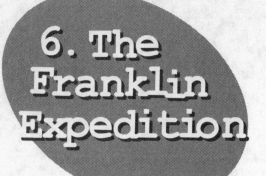

6. The Franklin Expedition

The mystery of the Franklin Expedition

The **Northwest Passage** between northern Canada and the Arctic is one of the most dangerous places for ships in the world. For centuries, navigators searching for a fast route to the Pacific tried to find a safe way of sailing through it. But the seas of northern Canada are treacherous, full of icebergs, jagged coastlines and pack ice waiting to trap unwary vessels. Indeed, so many ships and lives were lost that many people believed the Northwest Passage did not even exist.

Captain Sir John Franklin

Sir John Franklin, an early Governor of Tasmania, was sure the Northwest Passage could be found.

Route of the Franklin Expedition, 1845-46

When he returned to England from Australia in 1843, the
British Government chose him to lead two ships on an
expedition to northern Canada to look for it. Sir John was
overjoyed. He had spent years exploring the Arctic as a
young man, and had been knighted for his discoveries. The
government had promised him his expedition would be
equipped with all the most up-to-date navigation equipment
available. He knew that if anybody could find the Northwest
Passage, he could.

The Franklin Expedition set sail from England on 19 May,
1845. The two ships, *Erebus* and *Terror* were crewed by 128
men, and were lavishly fitted out. The ships' food supplies
even included a wonderful new invention: tinned food.

Thousands of
tins of meat
were stowed
in their holds
to feed the
hungry
sailors during
their months
at sea.

At first the
ships made
very good
progress. By

**H.M.S. *Erebus* and *Terror* leave London
for the Arctic**

July 1845 the expedition had reached Baffin Bay in northern
Canada and was heading west into uncharted seas. After that
nothing more was heard of it. For a while people in England
assumed that the expedition was proceeding as planned. But
when several years passed, and still no news arrived, the

authorities in England started to worry. Surely someone knew what had happened to Sir John and his men? Not until 1850 did they finally admit the truth. Sir John Franklin, two ships and 128 sailors had completely vanished.

The British Government sent rescue missions to Canada to see if any trace of the expedition could be found. The rescuers tracked the ships to Beechey Island in Lancaster Sound. Here hundreds of empty tin cans were found, proving the expedition had sheltered on the tiny island during the winter of 1845–46. Ominously, the searchers also found three graves. The tombstones, on a lonely spit of land, told the rescuers that sailors William Braine, John Torrington and John Hartnell had died in early 1846.

The searchers opened one of the graves to see if it contained any clues about the fate of the other men. To their surprise the body of Able Seaman John Hartnell was frozen solid, looking exactly as it had when it was buried. A doctor examined it, and decided Hartnell had probably died of tuberculosis, a dangerous lung disease. However, because the searchers were more interested in finding out what had happened to Sir John Franklin, at the time no more was thought of either the body, or its startling state of preservation. John Hartnell was put back into his coffin and reburied, deep in the icy ground.

The searchers sailed on, continuing to pick up equipment from the expedition, and occasionally finding the bones of dead sailors. Bit by bit, they pieced the sad fate of the expedition together. After leaving Beechey Island, the two ships had tried to sail south along the coast of King William Island, hoping to reach mainland Canada. If they had sailed down the east coast, they would have found the Northwest

Passage and the expedition would have been a success. Instead, Sir John Franklin took his ships down the west coast, straight into the icy Victoria Strait. Off the coast of King William Island, at a spot now called Starvation Cove, the ships sailed into ice and became stuck.

Some of the sailors were so hungry they turned into cannibals and ate each other, carrying supplies of their crew-mates' flesh in containers made from their boots.

In the months that followed Sir John Franklin and many of his men died. After being trapped in the ice for eighteen months, the remaining sailors abandoned the ships and set off, hoping to walk to civilisation. But the men were weak and food was short. Some of the sailors were so hungry they turned into cannibals and ate each other, carrying supplies of their crew-mates' flesh in containers made from their boots. Even these drastic efforts were in vain. The last survivors of the Franklin Expedition died in the lonely wastes of King William Island—sadly, leaving only 90 kilometres of the Northwest Passage still unmapped.

Activity:

Franklin Expedition snow goggles

Sir John Franklin's sailors were well equipped for the harsh arctic weather they knew they would encounter in their search for the Northwest Passage. Among the abandoned equipment later found by rescue missions were several pairs of snow goggles, used to keep the glare from bouncing off the ice into the men's eyes.

To make this copy of the Franklin Expedition snow goggles you will need some lightweight cardboard, coloured cellophane (light blue is particularly effective), pencils or felt pens, pins, glue, scissors and sticky tape.

INSTRUCTIONS

1. Photocopy or trace the patterns on page 75.
2. Fold the piece of cardboard in half. Cut carefully around your copy of the goggle pattern, remembering to cut out the eyes. Pin the pattern onto the cardboard so that the fold line sits on the fold in the cardboard and trace around the outside so that the pattern is transferred to the cardboard.
3. Remove the pattern. Cut around the tracing, holding the cardboard firmly together. (Be sure you make the goggle sides long enough to go around the back of your head.) When you have finished cutting, unpin the pattern and open out the fold. You should have a full pair of goggles.

4. Colour in and decorate the goggles.
5. Fold the cellophane in half, and pin the lens pattern to it. Cut around the lens pattern, being careful not to tear the cellophane.
6. Put glue on the back of the goggles, and stick the lenses into place.
7. Hold the goggles firmly in place, and get somebody else to sticky tape the ends together at the back of your head so that the goggles fit.

***Don't forget**—Your snow goggles are not sunglasses. If you try to use them in the glare you will hurt your eyes.*

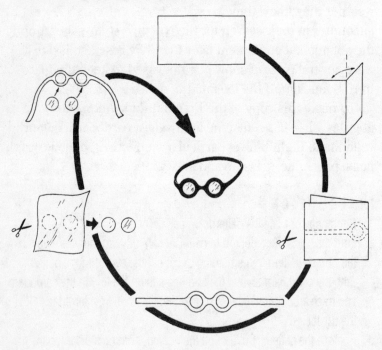

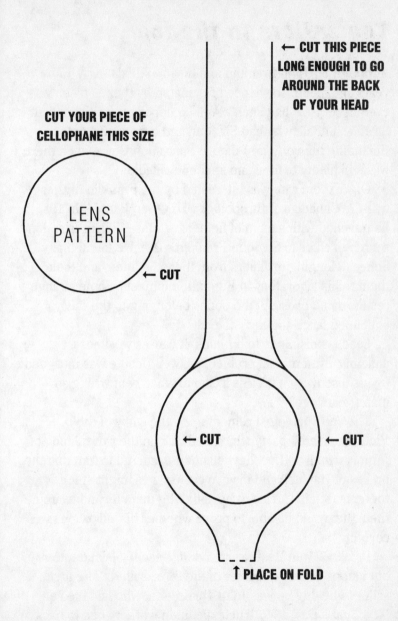

CUT YOUR PIECE OF
CELLOPHANE THIS SIZE

LENS
PATTERN

← CUT

← CUT THIS PIECE
LONG ENOUGH TO GO
AROUND THE BACK
OF YOUR HEAD

← CUT   ← CUT

↑ PLACE ON FOLD

The sailors in the ice

Although Sir John Franklin and his men died nearly 150 years ago, people have been fascinated by their sad story ever since. How had such a well-equipped expedition failed? Strangest of all, why had Sir John and twenty other men (including nine officers) died at Starvation Cove, when there was still plenty of food and shelter available?

One expert who was interested by the Franklin mystery was the Canadian anthropologist Dr Owen Beattie. In 1981 he travelled with a team of helpers to King William Island in search of clues to Sir John Franklin's fate. He found many bones belonging to sailors from the expedition, and took them to his laboratory in Edmonton for tests. Some strange results came back. All the bones belonging to the sailors contained large amounts of lead.

Lead is poisonous to humans. It causes weakness, anaemia, even mental problems. Owen Beattie was intrigued by his discovery. Was this a clue to what went wrong so many years ago?

The anthropologist remembered the story of the Victorian search party which had dug up the frozen body of John Hartnell on Beechey Island. It occurred to him that the bodies of Hartnell and his two crew-mates might still be there, frozen in the ice. If he could dig them up and examine them, he would be able to prove whether his suspicions were correct.

In 1984 Owen Beattie arrived on Beechey Island to carry out autopsies on the bodies of the three sailors. The first sailor to be dug up was John Torrington, who had died on New Year's Day, 1846. The expedition workers had to hack

through 1.5 metres of icy ground before they found him.
In the years since he had been buried, water had seeped into
John Torrington's coffin and frozen him into a coffin-shaped
iceblock. Owen Beattie and his helpers pulled off the coffin
lid and poured buckets of hot water over the ice to melt it.
At last they were able to pull aside
the dark blue cloth which covered
the dead sailor's face.

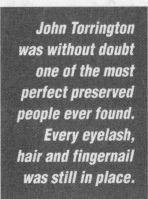

John Torrington was without doubt one of the most perfect preserved people ever found. Every eyelash, hair and fingernail was still in place.

An amazing sight met their
eyes: the thin, pale face and open
blue eyes of a young man who had
died 138 years before! Owen
Beattie could not have hoped for
better. John Torrington was
without doubt one of the most
perfect preserved people ever
found. Every eyelash, hair and fingernail was still in place.
His hands and feet, though white and waxy looking, might
have been those of a living person.

John Torrington had been a stoker on the *Terror*,
responsible for feeding the ship's boilers with coal. When he
died he was only twenty years old. Owen Beattie felt sad as
he looked at his body, but he knew that in a way, John
Torrington was lucky. By dying at the beginning of the
expedition, he had missed out on the horrors faced by his
ship-mates on King William Island. His body had been
carefully dressed in a striped shirt and trousers, and placed
in a specially made mahogany coffin. His death meant
something to his friends. By the time the last of his crew-
mates died three years later, nobody had the strength
to care.

An autopsy was carried out on John Torrington's body, proving he had probably died of pneumonia. However, his body had been strangely weakened before he died. Owen Beattie suspected lead poisoning. He took hair and tissue samples for testing and reburied the body in the ice. In 1986 the other two sailors, John Hartnell and William Braine were also dug up. Samples from all three sailors were taken back to Edmonton in Canada, together with ten ancient tin cans left by Franklin's men. Just as Owen Beattie had expected, the sailors' hair and tissues contained enormously high levels of lead, proving they had somehow contracted lead poisoning after leaving England.

The answer to the mystery was in the cans. Today, tin cans are made in factories by machines which work very precisely. However, in the 1840s the idea of canning food was still a new one. Early tin cans were handmade by tinsmiths, who shaped them around a cylindrical mould. The containers were made out of iron, but they were soldered shut with deadly lead solder.

JOHN TORRINGTON DIED JANUARY 1840 AGED 20 YEARS

This hand-painted coffin plate was found in Torrington's grave (it was probably made from one of the expedition's food cans)

Lead from the solder found its way into the food inside the cans and in turn gave the Franklin sailors lead poisoning. The evidence of the tins also helped explain why so many officers were among the first to die. The ordinary sailors ate the tinned meat only every second day, but the officers would probably have eaten it daily. The mystery of Sir John Franklin's death had been solved. He had been killed by the very modern technology he had hoped would help him conquer the frozen north.

Shelley's heart

The poet, Percy Shelley, drowned in a storm off the coast of Italy in 1822. His body was cremated on the beach in a special iron oven, but his heart refused to burn. It was souvenired by a friend. Later it was returned to his home in England, where his son would bring it out for visitors to admire. According to one unromantic family member, it looked like a piece of old boot leather.

The heart of another famous writer, Thomas Hardy, suffered a more undignified fate. According to one popular story, it was left to one side while his body was being prepared for burial—and was eaten by the cat.

7.
Head-
hunters

7. Head-hunters

The head-shrinkers

Since prehistoric times, head-hunters have existed in almost every continent. Armed with knives and machetes, they lurked in the steamy jungles of South America and New Guinea, and hid amongst the rocks of eastern European mountains. Some head-hunters were cannibals, who ate their victim's flesh. Others collected heads as war trophies, or gave them as offerings to the gods. Head-hunters believed that the head was the home of the dead person's soul, and that by cutting it off and keeping it, the owner had power over the ghost.

One South American people, the Jivaro Indians of Ecuador, not only collected human heads, but shrank them as well! The recipe for a shrunken head was gruesome and complicated. First, the dead person's head was cut off. The scalp and face were peeled away from the bones, and the skull and jaw bones were thrown away. Water was heated in a big cooking pot, and the skin and soft tissues were soaked for about two hours.

When the head was properly soaked, the head-shrinker took the pieces out of the pot and sewed them back together. The eyes and mouth were also sewn shut so that the head looked like a floppy skin balloon. Hot stones were pushed into the neck opening. The heat drew the moisture out of the tissues, and the head slowly began to shrink. By removing the stones and replacing them with a series of smaller ones, the head-shrinker could shrink it until it was no bigger than a doll's head.

When the last stones were removed, the head-shrinker filled the head with hot sand. He lit a fire, and hung the head from a tripod made of sticks so that it could cure in the smoke. (This was usually done overnight.) Finally, the brown, shrivelled head was painted to make it look more attractive. It could then be added to the head-shrinker's grisly collection of trophies.

Musical bones

The Inca people had a novel way of preserving their enemies' bodies. They turned them into musical instruments! The skin was used to make war drums, and the shin bones were turned into flutes.

The Incas also used their enemies' skulls as cups. Another person who had a skull cup was the poet, Lord Byron. He used it to drink claret—a dark red wine which looks like blood.

The Scottish head-hunter

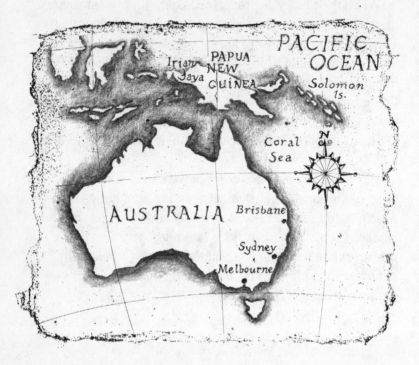

For many years, shrunken heads were popular exhibits in European museums. Explorers went to South America especially to collect them, and ships returning from New Zealand brought preserved Maori heads (prized for their beautiful tattoos) back to white 'head-hunters' in Europe.

Today, museums no longer collect heads. But visitors to one museum in Scotland can still see an exhibit which is as gruesome as it is fascinating, and behind which is one of the most remarkable stories about head-hunters ever told.

In 1875 an Australian ship, the *Bobtail Nag*, called into the island of Malaita in the Solomon Islands. While the ship was at anchor, a native came aboard and handed its captain a piece of wood with a message on it—a message written in English! The captain quickly sent some men ashore to investigate. To their surprise they found a Scottish sailor called John Renton, who had lived with a tribe of head-hunters for over seven years!

Renton's adventure was a strange one. According to the tale he told the captain, he and four other sailors had run away from a ship called the *Reynard* in a small boat, hoping to find an island paradise in the South Seas. For weeks they drifted on the Pacific. Storms blew them off course, and they were so hungry that the other men were ready to kill Renton and eat him. Fortunately, they managed to catch a shark and eat it instead. At last the boat reached the Solomon Islands where they were found and taken care of by natives.

The four other sailors died, but Renton survived because he was young and strong. He became a member of the Asi tribe. The Asi believed that when a person died, their spirit continued to live in their head. They collected human heads, and filled their homes with

> *The Asi believed that when a person died, their spirit continued to live in their head. They collected human heads, and filled their homes with skulls belonging to their ancestors.*

skulls belonging to their ancestors. Renton became a head-hunter too. He joined the Asi's expeditions against their enemies, and helped preserve the heads on special racks in the village. Kabau, the chief's son, became his friend and gave him a necklace made of human teeth. By the time of the *Bobtail Nag's* arrival, the Scottish sailor was a valued and respected member of the tribe.

After his rescue Renton went back to his home town of Stromness in the Orkney Islands, where he gave his tooth necklace to a friend. (It later made its way into the Scottish National Museum of Antiquities.) But Scotland was cold and bleak. Renton could not forget the Pacific islands where he had lived for so many years, and soon he returned to sea. In 1878, while sailing with a ship called the *Mystery*, the Scottish head-hunter was killed in an ambush on the island of Aoba in Vanuatu. His body was roasted and eaten by cannibals—and his head was stuck on a pole.

The convict's fingers

Life as a convict in the 1820s was always hard, particularly under the brutal Captain Logan in the settlement of Moreton Bay. One convict was so anxious to get out of work he chopped off his own fingers. The fingers can be seen to this day—preserved in a bottle in the Museum of the Royal Queensland Historical Society.

8. Frozen for the Future

8. Frozen for the Future

Cryonics

Everybody has heard of Tutankhamun and the Iceman. But who has heard of Doctor James Bedford? A psychology teacher from California, Dr Bedford may one day be as famous as the other preserved people in this book. When he died in December 1967 at the age of 73, Dr Bedford was not buried or cremated. Instead he arranged for his body to be frozen in **liquid nitrogen**, so that he could be defrosted far in the future and brought back to life.

The practice of freezing dead people for the future is known as **cryonics**. By having their bodies frozen, some people believe that they will have a second chance at life. They hope that hundreds of years from now doctors will be able to cure them of whatever they died of. Nobody will ever die, and frozen people from the past will be resurrected to lead happy and useful lives in an ideal future society.

The idea of freezing dead bodies is an American one. It was first promoted in the mid-1960s by a man called

Robert Nelson. Several cryonics companies now operate in the United States, mostly on the west coast. People who want to be frozen wear a tag around their neck, so that if they die in the street the cryonics company can collect their bodies quickly. (This is important, because once the body starts to decay the chances of bringing it back to life are not as good.) Cryonics companies also offer a cheaper service to poorer people who cannot afford the high costs of keeping their body frozen. They cut off the person's head and freeze it

> *Cryonics companies also offer a cheaper service to poorer people who cannot afford the high costs of keeping their body frozen. They cut off the person's head and freeze it separately.*

separately. People who do this hope that as long as their brain is preserved, their head can be attached to another body like Frankenstein's creature, or even to a sophisticated robot.

Not everybody is so optimistic about the frozen people's chances. Frozen people run the risk that even in the future doctors will not be able to resurrect them. Another problem is that it is difficult to be sure the cryonics company will stay in business long enough for the bodies to be brought back to life. Fifty years from now someone may well get tired of wasting power and nitrogen on a room full of frozen heads and simply turn off the refrigerator. Already some cryonics companies have gone bankrupt, and all the bodies in their care have been defrosted.

People who are against cryonics also point out that frozen

twentieth-century humans may not enjoy life in the distant future. They say that everything will have changed so much that it will be impossible for the defrosted people to adapt. All their friends and relations will be dead, and they will be lonely and afraid.

To get some idea of how a defrosted person might feel, imagine that twentieth-century doctors could bring the Iceman back to life. The Iceman lived 5000 years ago in an isolated village, probably in a tiny hut. He dressed in skins, and ate animals he hunted himself with a bow and arrows. What would he make of cars, computers, modern skyscrapers forty storeys tall? How would he cope with clothes made by machines and food packaged in plastic? Who could he talk to in a language that disappeared thousands of years ago? How would he feel knowing most people were interested in him as a curiosity who should be in a museum?

Nevertheless people continue to be frozen, hoping, just as the ancient Egyptians did, that their bodies will live on after death. Already, they point out, test-tube babies have been born from fertilised eggs which were frozen and stored until needed. Whatever happens, it is at least a possibility that in the far future some archaeolgist will discover the frozen people, and be excited to learn what twentieth-century people were really like.

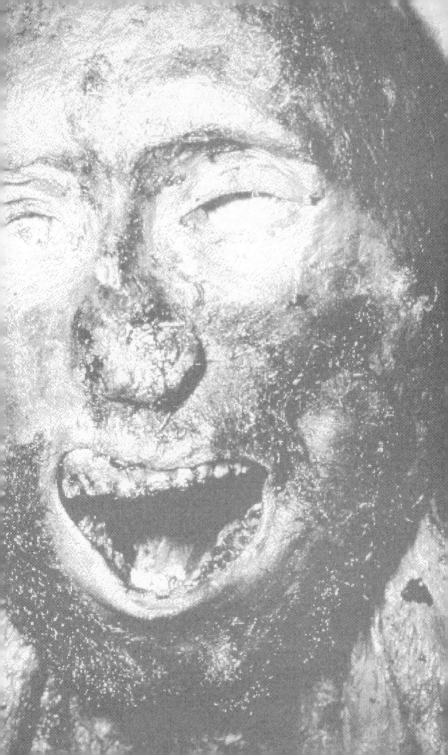

Glossary

amulet: an object worn to ward off evil spirits; a protecting charm

anthropologist: a person who studies the origins and development of humankind

antiquary: an expert on ancient things

archaeologist: a person who studies cultures, especially ancient ones, by excavating and piecing together their remains

autopsy: the examination and dissection of a body after death, in order to find out more about it, and to decide what caused the death

botanist: a scientist who studies plants and plant groups

carbon dating: a process used to determine the age of plants or animals by measuring how much radioactive carbon they contain

crypt: an underground chamber, often beneath the floor of a church, used as a burial place

Druid: a person belonging to an order of ancient Celtic priests of Britain, Ireland and France

Egyptologist: a person who studies ancient Egyptian culture and artefacts

embalm: to treat a dead body with potions, spices etc (and today with drugs or chemicals) in order to preserve it from decay

mummy: the dead body of a human being or an animal preserved by a method of embalming

pharaoh: an ancient Egyptian king

pilgrim: a person who journeys long distances to visit a holy place

sacrifice: to offer life or material possessions to a god or goddess in the hope that this will bring good fortune

shaman: a priest or witchdoctor who claims to have supernatural powers

Tutankhamun: an Egyptian king of the Eighteenth Dynasty (fourteenth century BC). His treasure-filled tomb was discovered near Luxor by Howard Carter in 1922

Further Reading

If you would like to find out more about preserved people, the following books will help you. Most of them are recently published, and should be available in public libraries; if not, ask your librarian to get them in for you. Some of the books were written for grown-ups. I have marked these with an asterisk, but you should still find them interesting.

Unfortunately, there are no books available yet on the St Bees knight. However, photographs of the knight appear in Don Brothwell's book, mentioned below.

BOG BODIES

The bog man and the archaeology of people
by Don Brothwell
(British Museum Publications, London, 1986)
(This interesting book has lots of pictures, and covers preserved people from all over the world, as well as bog bodies.)

* *The bog people: Iron Age man preserved*
by P.V. Glob
(Faber, London, 1969)

THE FRANKLIN EXPEDITION

Buried in ice: the story of a lost Arctic expedition
by Owen Beattie and John Geiger
(Ashton Scholastic, Toronto, 1992)

* *Frozen in time : the fate of the Franklin Expedition*
by Owen Beattie and John Geiger
(Bloomsbury, London, 1987)

EGYPTIAN MUMMIES

Mummies, masks and mourners
by Margaret Berrill
(Hamish Hamilton, London, 1989)
(This book also covers other preserved people including Lindow Man, and the Greenland mummies.)

Ancient Egypt: a civilization project book
by Susan Perdy and Cass R. Sandak
(Franklin Watts, 1982)
(An activity book full of ancient Egyptian artefacts, including instructions on how to make a pyramid, a queen's headdress, and an amulet with your name in hieroglyphs.)

Mummies, tombs and treasure: secrets of ancient Egypt
by Lila Perl
(Clarion Books, 1987)

THE ICEMAN

* *The man in the ice*
by Konrad Spindler
(Weidenfeld & Nicholson, London, 1994)

JOHN RENTON, THE SCOTTISH HEAD-HUNTER

* *White Headhunter*
by Hector Holthouse
(Angus and Robertson, Sydney, 1988)

94

Index

If you enjoyed this book, you'll want to read more *True Stories...*

An exciting new series of high-interest, easy-to-read paperbacks for kids who want more than glossy pictures and captions in their non-fiction. This is narrative non-fiction in which real-life stories—from the sensational to the serious; from biography to history; sport to the supernatural—come alive on the page.

A great blend of entertainment and information, with illustrations, colour photos, and things to make and do.

MONSTERS AND CREATURES OF THE NIGHT
by Sue Bursztynski
Vampires and zombies; werewolves and water monsters...the creatures of the night who haunt our dreams...The truth about Dracula, Frankenstein's creature, zombies, the Loch Ness monster, and many others, is revealed in this ghoulish collection of true stories. Full of fascinating legends, and real-life sightings.

STOKED! *Real Life, Real Surf*
by Glyn Parry
Rip into surfing's hottest adventures. Meet starry people who surf. Filth locations, radical moves, spacey equipment, hardcore action...*Stoked!* will speedline you straight into stoke heaven!

INCREDIBLE JOURNEYS *Adventures into the Unknown*
by Rick Wilkinson
It's not too late to go exploring—there's plenty left to discover and do. Remarkable true stories of heroes of the air like Charles Kingsford-Smith, lone sailors like Kay Cottee, mountaineers, cavers, jungle explorers, and many others, bring the world of modern exploration to life.

And coming soon...

Antarctica:
the Cruellest Place on Earth
by John Nicholson

Love Rules!
by Pamela Freeman

Mysterious Ruins
by Natalie Jane Prior

Flashes of Gold: Women in Sport
by Margrete Lamond